For Daryl Ruth Orians,

All best,

Rodolphe Squires
Ann Arbor, 1967

*The Light Under Islands*

# The
# Light
# Under
# Islands

*Poems by*

Radcliffe Squires

*Ann Arbor*
The University of Michigan Press

Earlier, and in some instances radically different, versions of some of these poems have appeared in the following journals: *Accent, Anon, Aspen, Hika,* the *New York Times, Poetry, The Sewanee Review,* and *The Western Humanities Review.* Acknowledgment is gratefully made to the respective editors.

*For Eileen*

# Contents

# *Two  on  a  Motorcycle*

Fitted like sleepers together
In cautious parallels, the leather
Ones barely touch. Remote as aquarium scenes their
    faces peer
Through the burning blue plastic spheres
Of their helmets as they weave on the skate
Edge of momentum, sleepers held bolt upright
By a blue dream. Where are they going,
Wordless and shrunk back into a leather sheath
    like a stallion's
Sex?

    May love set them face to face,
May shame fragment them into speech.
God send them no more summer but error to break
Their perfection, unsheathe, shake
Them from their dream of blurred spokes
That suddenly stop. And then the long arc
Of their bodies catapulted through the dark
Blue air in sleeper's formation toward a dower
Of earth, blue, always to be blue, but the color
    of no flower.

## Midwestern Portrait

By morning he fishes the green vein
Of the meadow stream between
His traps. His adolescent hand shakes
As he feels the trout play with the bait.
All his body hisses "now" and sets
The shank in bone and cartilage.

He peers at the fish in the shadowy creel.
Its fins flag a sprig of mint. He feels
Its comfort lag against his thigh.

Later the trapped otter stares into his eyes
And, seeing the wild kinship there,
Pours forth its sexual smell like tears.

At night the smell of exultation and despair
Still comes from his hand as he drives his baited car
Through the amber traps of semaphores.
His face blurs between his dark font of hair
And his T shirt's shrill, reflexive white.
He tunes his radio across the arc of night
Until he finds his music.

                              O, it's the head
Of Hugh of Lincoln singing over his lapsing blood.
Furred by pain, young and small,
It can hardly be understood coming up from the well.
But it comes. You don't have,
It cries, to get caught by life,

2

You don't need to get trapped by a book.
This welling blood on which I float will do
For both. Its name is the same for a boy
Or a girl. "Baby." Blood-baby, baby. Blood hurts
But it doesn't bore.

                    Between the spurts
Of voice, eight pistons in epidermis of oil and veed
Like a weight lifter's latissimus spread
Say everything else that needs to be said.

## Midway

Even at night
Now hardly is any place that
You cannot hear the great
Highways. Inhaling, until the refrigerated van
Passes the ear's meridian and then
Exhaling into the direction of directions.
And the breaths crossing like instruments
In a dreamed music. Music of weight
Pressed on air, pressed on rubber, splayed
On asphalt. Oh, music of a land
Disinhabited by the music played on gray bands,
Music of the migrations of metal hordes
Glittering in a memory of movement, moving towards
The sameness of a road unreeling like space
Ahead of motion. Space, movement. No house,
No barn corrupts this ultimate wilderness.
You can only exit from such a paradise
Into imaginable Fargos, predictable Laramies,
Those fallen worlds of food and lodgings,
Those human rigmaroles, those needless pageants.

I exit through a South Dakota night
Into a town called Midway. It has dried
In its exile below the highway.
The buildings lean shilly-shally,
Slatted and wavering like a snowfence
On the street, the glass dim as cobwebs

And lightless. What once was a spa still
From its flaking darkness yields the smell
Of geyser water. Imagine: princely ranch hands,
Their necks like tooled morocco bands
Above their long white underwear bodies,
Taking the sulphurous waters
Amid the poplar-racked cornfields of Dakotas!
But that's gone if it ever was,
A board nailed over it crosswise,
In the darkness under a loud
Highway whose headlights overshoot
The brink of the hill.
                              I park and walk
To the one lighted window shoved against the dark.

I drink the dank waiter's coffee in the dishwater glare
And then I feel the door open and hear
A coin fall into a slot, fingers of a juke box stir.
I turn before the music starts and stare
Into the faces of youths who would as lief
Knife me as talk to me, would rather, perhaps, save
They have something better to do—to stand near to,
Without ever quite touching, their hero.
He is an Indian.

                    What was it, a hundred
And thirty years ago that first steamboat floundered
Up the Missouri to the headwaters of the Yellowstone?

5

Catlin the painter stared like a lens
From the deck. The sidewheel dug the catfish
Water, and sparks from the funnel ravished
The prairie grass. And all the Indians of the Dakotas,
Blackfeet, Piegans, the Bloods, Gros Ventres,
Stood on the shores, speaking in dead voices.
They saw their future become someone else's.
It belonged to the builders of the boats
That walked on water. To the builders of roads
On water, to the builders of roads.

And now, below these roads that connect
No town with any other, that intersect
With nothing but themselves, this underlife
Turns from any future, turns smiling to the knife,
To the wicked song and the dangerous odor—
The odor of grass burned over and rained over—
That strains through the denim mesh.
And to the smile that is less in the flesh
Than the deep bone pattern where even the blood
Is made and where life, when it must, as it must,
Will turn and stand at bay. Here below the soft-
Hoofed stampede. In a pocket below the roads.

# Nebraska, Perhaps

The highway at dusk becomes
An aluminum arabesque of clovers,
Mergings and overpasses,
And the churring wheels pull
Me suddenly into a future
Whose gleaming order and law
Freeze in the fantastic perfection
Of a final madness. Faltering, I look up
Where turquoise fog lights are coming on,
Not because there is fog but because
A photo cell has noted the sunset's fading.
And I see at the very zenith
Of the overpass a child holding
A fishing pole sternly over the road.

Is he fishing for cars?

O, to be caught by a child!
To be brought up, I and this car struggling
At the end of a thin translucent line!
To be lifted by a thin brown arm held together
By its weaknesses. To be raised by a child
Into the fog lights opening now
Like pale blue Mongolian eyes.

It is not much, this, to go on,
But it fills me with wild courage.
I glide under the colossal bridge-legs of the child,
And my foot sinks lovingly into the accelerator.

7

# John the Baptist

                                    He came
Along the street and asked me where a church
Was he could preach at. I just stood
Trying to think of a bright thing to say,
When suddenly I saw he had little rags
Of light around him—not quite, but almost like
A picture angel's. From behind his smile
He twisted up at me; lavender lips
Lolled about tobacco yellow teeth.
And the faultless, amber nails like five almonds
At his lapel. Before I could say anything
He spoke again. "Guess you wouldn't know, son,
About a church. I'll find one, though, myself.
I always do. I'm John the Baptist. The same
As in the Bible. I've never died. Never will."

It wasn't what he said. That was only
Crazy. It wasn't the way he said it.
That was only lazy and southern-cute.
It was that he so gently yet proudly exposed his madness.
Not to invite me in for an experiment
In the high temperatures of his logic, but
To lay waste my soul before I had his.

All that day in streets I saw
Gray ice swelling from the sockets of eyes.
Smiles turned upside down, thin as wire at the ends.
I heard gossiping between souls.
And rising over all the exultation of the holy addict.

After that day I did not see or feel those things.
I never saw John the Baptist again.
But if you've once looked into
The blind spot of God you don't have
To look again to know it's there.

# *Friendship*

We are fourteen and fishing
In a just plain rotten canal. Our fallen bicycles
Twist up on one horn like skeletons of bison.
The wet from the bank mud feeds
A low current through our pants,
Murmuring that we are not the ones spent
Good money for those clothes.
The perch we've caught (and would not dare
Take home) work their gills and stare
At the sun. From time to time one
Tantrums, fluttering in the air.
Their smell and the smell of worms
Are on our hands, and blood
And the funeral smell
Of the water. Yet our
Hands keep touching, sharing
Their degradation as the sun
Moves down through our shoulders toward the cold
Wet rot coming up through our thighs
From the mud. And our hands
Keep touching. Indeed, my friend
Grows ridiculously tender.
He drops his head on my shoulder,
His eyes sluing sideways through the lattice
Of his lashes. He keeps saying my name,
Trying on progressively sadder
Diminutive endings. Until suddenly

10

He says very calmly, "You know what?
I'm turning into a woman,"
Adding as he opens his shirt, "But
So far, just on one side."
Though one breast is darkly swollen
It is more like a bruise
Than a metamorphosis.
Still, the nipple does stick out like a wicked little tongue.
We are both horrified and proud
Of that flesh which he covers again
Like a jewel, saying as if it were
Some mountainous irrelevance, "We'll always
Be friends, won't we?" I have
Visions of being stuck for life with this freak.
I see others sauntering cruel and cool
Through the noon halls of the school
While my friend and I hide in a corner
With hard boiled eggs, crumbling sandwiches
And his melodramatic disease.
But I find myself nodding "yes."

I do not believe he turned into a woman.
But I do not know. We could never bring
Ourselves to talk together again.
We had not learned yet never to say
Or ask or give as much as is needed
And so used up our friendship in one day.

# The Athletes

"Listen, Lykos," Pharos said to me
As I undressed, thinking hard about
The race. You remember Pharos. Three
Years ago he almost won but hasn't run again.
"Listen, Lykos," Pharos said. "I came
To wish you luck. I think you'll win today.
Something about you says you've left
No room for losing. Still, it was like that, too,
For me one year. Yet, just as I felt
The ice cold arms of that austere twin of ours
In his pale, future cell, the winner passed me.
As I waited for my pulse to come back to
Present time, I watched the winner borne
On the shoulders of friends whose love smeared
The burnish of dust into his sweat. They bore
Him toward his statue, toward his poem
That the Theban poet writes before the races,
Leaving the name and the usual lies
About ancestors to be added later.
And I saw how the eyes of all the watchers
Followed the winner toward the moment
That stops in white paint on historical bronze
When an athlete is proclaimed the winner.
But then I saw the watchers watched me also,

Covertly, with some sad but infinite
Greed. Secretly they bore me into the twilight
Of hovels where small lamps smoke, bracing
For the crush of night. Even now, dear Lykos,
As I speak, they carry me away, far
From my statue, my poem, my cruel-faced twin,
And into the temple that is never finished
Where in silence adorers proclaim me the loser.'

## The Herring Gull

Except for nesting times
His life is only these climbs
And falls. The slow soaring
To the height that abstracts herring
To a boiling of sea-surface. The descent
Into a marvelous but baffling element.

Again and again,
Until he can rise to fall no more
And, edged by tides up the metamorphic shore,
Is stopped at last by little shells,
A reed, a pebble. Sand half-fills
The coves of his wings, and all
The wind-polished feathers splay and curl
Like seed heads of grass. And though his beak
Still gapes toward a brightness where herring break
The surface, it is not to ask for more.
One idea was enough; one metaphor.
Enough that after all assaults are finished
The cold trouble still seethes undiminished.

## The Young Poet at Bluff, Utah

Dawn is the ancient silence that slips
Into rocks. In the beginning there is no word.
There is the half-human smell of the dead sage fire,
The mineral stink of the car under dust,
The smell of his friend, their sleeping bag, himself.

Ugh! To leave it all, to stand
Naked and cold, aimed like light
Toward the source of light.

Where light is turned toward light,
The lizard is frozen halfway
Toward the fly locked in the amber
Of its air. The glittering grain of pollen hangs
Above a shining orifice. The black oars
Of the turtle rest in the motionless river.
These are the only images. Drifting
Like hawks in the germ cell, they make
The million faces of God.

He stands naked and cold and feels
His freedom close in on him.
He feels light disappear in light and says,
"Move, dangerous sun,
Come to the shore, black turtle,
Black lexicon. Whatever words
I speak are spoken across your
River, and you bear them.

Whatever syntax joins them
Joins the mercator projections of your armor."

He says, "Move, sun. Take the fly, lizard.
My words are the blinking of your eyes."

He says, "Move, sun. Fall, pollen. Burn like a meteor
In that heavy atmosphere.
My words are your burning."

He says, "Move, dangerous sun, and move
Me with you. Move the seed
In my flesh; my cannibal enzymes move.
Move the waste rivers of my life.
At each pore set a fountain
Where rainbows form at the rainbow's end.
Give me back my prison walls
Where the flat human voice
Of my friend will blunder
As he wakes full of the self-pity of sleep
And cries, 'Build up the fire, for Jesus' sake!' "

# Caravaggio at the Quarry of Paradise

The ancient quarry at Syracuse was worked by slaves, later by prisoners. The modern name, *Latomia del Paradiso,* is said to have been bestowed by the seventeenth-century painter Caravaggio.

Wherever the wise and good have walked and plotted
Monuments—those rosy fountains in a square,
Ramps of travertine, steps rising between lions
To a library—there the mad and wicked come. There
The drifter pauses, selling sunlight. Naked
To the doctoral moon stands the transvestite.
Through the bodies of scholars spurt
The schools of child-rake illiterates.

In a square like a mirage of stone
Upon black unmoving water I found
The priest who has no priestly duty. Ruin
Of priests, he lies naked like Bacchus in the vine shadows
At the corners of the eye, foot in a halo of dust
Raised to caress the whirlpool of grapes.
In the small room back of the nerve's wine house
He sits like the knowledge of a hidden birthmark,
Albuminous flesh pressed by indolent fruit, all
The eyes of grapes in the whirlpools
Of his hair. When I sheathed my knife
In a gaming heart, feeling the pulse
Lift the blade, this priest stared at us like a bird.
The stage beyond his eyes had finally
Played the drama behind his eyes.

17

Not from the crime but from his cold approval
I fled. From the sallow gold of the plaza
Whose perfection draws forth a perfect
Ignobility. From the pale flesh gazing
Through the bars of its perfection. From the pale
Plaza staring through the lines of itself.
                              Here at Syracuse
A Judas tree has traced its red veins
Against the sky. Like a drawing
By Vesalius it stands
Within itself, untroubled by meaning.
Below it are the quarries. Those caverns
Whose stone was cut away by
Soft flesh. Centuries of prisoners, like ants.
No plan. No noble purpose.
Here one trespasses
Pink or green surfaces
Gleaming like viscera under a skin of water.
One cavern is like another, the beautiful
Absence where stone has been taken away.
If there is music, it is a music heard
Only by itself, stone music for a stone ear.
Flight, like Oedipal Athens, ends here.
In the prisoner's freedom.
In the blind sockets of rocks.
In the anatomical drawing on the sky.

# The Etruscans and Us

The children are left to play outside the tomb
Because, as the guide says, of the paintings
Of "profane love." Prepared to seem unprepared
We descend the steep stair down to the airless room
Where the lovers painted on the wall await
Like a red meadow for our breath to graze.
And though we are smiling and feeling our purses,
We find in the hush that we have after all
Gone like other travelers below the earth and have to ask
The old questions, "What was it you did not do?
Why did your life fail?"

Vulnerable in their space these lovers
Give themselves not to each other
But to their act. Sadly they suffer each other
For that act's sake. And so, while they are as flat
And small as life they are not life.
We should not believe them in life. We believe them here.
By giving no answer they are an answer.
What they give by not giving is the knowledge
That a bad art, like a bad life, is an art that almost succeeds;
And a great art, like a great life, is one that almost fails.

Meanwhile, thank God, the children
Are running hard in the flowers
On top of our heads.

# Dear Hercules, Dear Twin

## I

*A Birth at Thebes*

Where I lay in the city a world sloped away,
Hushed, delaying beginnings, prolonging ends.
The tricked nurse with her fingers locked open
Stood like a column. I mused on serious God;
On the steaming chasm I pythoned through;
On the groves of oak where I could wander
As an enigma to be understood
By enigmas that I should almost understand.
But why and in what way? Was I the son
Whose cudgel-destiny hung in uncut stone
Like a marble headache? Was I the one who
Looking up never saw sky, but always the face
Of Anteus growing smaller, grayer and suddenly
Too wise? Or was I, as I think, the son who wakes
And thinks himself blind because the light
Is the color of his own eyes? That light—
When thin frost thins at dawn and the ichor
Of the field burns in the milk, *that* light.

In that light the serpents eddied.

Serpents are doubtless a father's testing,
His suspicion that some god begot the child.
His supreme suspicion must be reverenced,
The serpents throttled and tossed at his feet

20

So he will not be cheated of his joy
At having been divinely cheated.

Serpents are doubtless a mother's testing,
Her suspicion that some god did not beget the child.
For her sake the serpents must be caressed,
Cajoled to circle your arms and kiss
Your temples, then to dart their black lightning
In your ears. Ever afterward you will
Understand important matters—the speech of vultures,
    for example.
For vultures, those heavy shadows, are the most
Innocent of creatures, never having harmed
A living thing. And what else is there to do
But narrow the circle, lower the altitude on death?

I, in the lit silence of that room,
Murderer and priest, strangler
And vulture, I vomited, oh
Mother, your milk across my father's
Sky. See, there we are, the pale
Silhouette of us among the clambering planets,
As I scream for myself, waking all
The city into the turbulence, my turbulence
That has to happen now.

I I

*A Murder of Children*

From that chamber I walked toward
A darker chamber. The darkest. My way was through
Gymnasiums of the sun. Light everywhere coming down
As a mild blue swimmer into mountain towns.
Light coming up as a new presence into
The dust where the cattle and the herdsmen
Drifted, scattering like boats through squalls
Of light. My way was through stoas
Of love. The youths who are always
Pretending to wrestle stood gravely apart
As I walked through white arguments toward
The darkest chamber. The girls—who lift me
With sea murmurs in the field and afterward weep
In a forest of frightened families—smiled
A long while into their own faces as
They drew water from the well.

Love is twelve ways of almost anything,
But in the end love is the faceless figure
Who stands beyond a certain archway
In the city. You do not have to enter the arch,
But if you do, you must follow the slow steps
That you cannot overtake.
Down streets of artisans you will follow

And you alone will see the distant figure
That pauses only when you think
With some relief that now surely
It will disappear. And you will go on
Past linens and figs, brushing aside
The tradesmen and beggars like curtains
Until you see the figure turn into
A side street where you know the face
Will be open at last to you. When
You also turn into that street there is not
Even the sound of sandals or the shutting of
A door. The street is all doors, all the same,
And all of them shut, and at the end
Rises the archway beyond which your self,
Or twin self, is waiting, staring at you.

And just as you would say, "So that was it,"
The password will not come.
Ice forms upon the glance held too long,
And the twin turns bellowing upon
Whatever is near; what is nearest,
Sons, daughters, crying, "Ah, how good,
How good!" as his steel hands tear their bellies
Open, and the light, this being the way of light,
Peers impartially at their similar lavender guts.

The roads of the world stretch into the ash
Gray hills where the shepherd carries

An unsure lamb over his shoulder. They stretch
Into the bronze plains where a girl
Drags home arbutus branches.
White oxen move like white oxen on
The roads. But at the point where the
Roads all come together, there is the moment
Where the husband screams with the wounds he has
Given his children. Here the tornado puts down
Its toe. The only way out is by going in farther.

III

*An Oracle at Delphi*

As a ship dragged by storms onto a rock
Must wait for storms to float it free
I waited in the darkest chamber. I was
Born once, I thought; that is, I had
Been mortally wounded and was certain, therefore,
To live. Now, must I be born again?

No answer came, but the answer may always be
The silence of the chamber, the silence
Growing in the mouth of the cold volcano,
Rounded at last like a refused kiss
Pressed on air. Or, the answer may be
Neither silence nor sound, but the darkness
In the throat of the cold volcano
Where nothing living grows, but stone grows;

24

Where roots—that do not feed—stab darkness,
Where stems—that do not drink—pierce
Darkness. And the glittering flowers, the heavy
Snowflakes of the sun, the flowers that do not
Breed, slowly turn, turning their faces
Slowly but at last fully to the darkness,
To the silence, to the coldness.
                                    Except
You enter the kingdom of hell you cannot
Be born again.
                    No one was glad
That I came into the world again, this
Time not with baby's eyes still vacant
And lolling on the tide, but with eyes
That quickly clamped down on the light.

I stood then and went between the no and yes
Of every king, rising through spring irises
Until I came into the mountain which once
In search of itself rose from the sea floor
Bearing a dolphin into the dry thin height.
Below, wild olive like puffs of smoke
Blew into a mist moving from a sea
Made more patiently blue by the loss of a mountain.
Above, wild olive like falling ash flaked
The final red color of the cliffs thrust
Into a sky made less certainly blue

By the presence of a dolphin forever sighing into
A lesser color. I gazed at the temples swaying on their
African legs halfway between the streets
Of the courtesans and the place of the athletes.
Between the temples I found the pythoness.
Her serpents tasted the air between us.
"Well," she said, "you are not like the rest,
The impotent who want to know how
To bring life into the world; the potent
Who want to know how to bring death."
A silence. Then, as one who is underpaid and in
A hurry, she spoke rapidly, dully, her eyes somewhere else.
"You must change your name. Choose a name with irony,
One that praises your enemy. You must
Change your city. Choose a city you hate,
Not very beautiful and not too important,
Ruled by a king you despise. Be
His slave. That is one way of
Becoming a god, and the only way for
Those who are stupid." For awhile
She mused then touched herself not
At all decently and laughed high above
The air where her words were fading.

IV

*A Little Farm at Tiryns*

From the walls of a city not very beautiful,
Not too important, I watched new wheat
Come like the sudden catastrophe of a green puberty.
Parsley wove from comatose soil
A net that crowded birds and suns
Together in a glistening element
Where everything that ever happened happens
Again. And I saw the courtesy of
The earth: most in repose when most busy.

A first bee stuttered on a flowerless land,
Striking not-yet-flowers. Him I
Followed into the absolute harvest.
I went into the cyclamen that is
Always a whiteness in the deep frost
Of the mountains, always a nectar
Among desiccated leaves, a storm
Of pollen in the hard, unmoving winter.

I went into the absolute river, into the crystal
Of ice whose paralysis floods all banks,
Dissolves all mountains and carries the evidence
Of itself forever to the sea.

Through the gut of a worm I went into

The absolute earth. Through the fur of a root
I went into the earth that tolerates the
Worm and the root, the river, the harvest
And moves nothing, holds nothing, but
Moves itself, holds itself.
                              I held
The earth upon my back, the smell
Of ferns like milk; the beaks of flowers
Deep in my skin; the rivers flowing
In my hair. I held this earth
Until on my hand grew three apples,
Whirling in their bloom of yeasts
Upon my palm where sunlight
Anxiously watched my moisture ooze
From the pores and make all the rainbows.

This is the harvest become harvest.
It cannot be kept. This is the harvest
That is given back as an earnest to an earth
That cannot be held up forever.

V

*Goodbye, Hylas*

The oar snaps, and the boat nuzzles
The weed-soft rocks of a particular island.
Before you leave the boat, before you step ashore,
Your downy faced excuse abandons you.
He had always been there. When you killed,
His unformed voice said it was only a joke
That had somehow gone too far.
When your hand, cold beneath its light fur,
Went hunting beneath the robes of someone's wife,
He smiled like a cup bearer who is a bit
Clumsy for having grown fast, yet still
Too young to know what the pinches mean
As he moves naked among the drinkers.
And when you loosed the chariot upon the games,
And the crowd went suddenly silent,
It was his body that leaned away
From the wheel that leaned away. He had
No confidence in the one thing that all are sure
Of. Dust made drowsy tracks in the moist trough
Of his breast, red roads on his eyes.

I watched without belief or disbelief
As he stepped from the boat, bearing
A pitcher. For awhile seen like light moving behind

The oak leaves, then only the oak leaves, their
Shadows behind their shadows. Then
I called his name. Too late. What is always here
Can never hear you. It is always too late when
You come to the spring in the forest on
A particular island, where three women stand
In the twilight, their bodies tall and
Transparent, their eyes pale blue, their hair as gray
As ice.
          "He suffered not at all," they said,
"But smiled as we took back this or that,
Which after all we gave him. One part
At a time. Those broad hands. One at a time.
And the rest. He was, you know, nothing
But extremities. He who had come from water,
Came for water. Water he got. Suffer
He did not." Their words were soft,
But their unchanging stare was what that lady
Turned to the musician who looked back
Over his unlucky shoulder with the mischievous
Abjection of a philosopher who has changed his mind.
But theirs not the stare of the cheated;
Theirs was the long look that says, "I
Shall be waiting for you on the plains of Thrace."

Then they were gone.

And the boat was gone, comrades gaily gone
Toward other islands. I stood alone on an island,
Gazing down on a pitcher of clear water,
Myself a little more than water.

V I

*How to Measure a Race Course*

An island draws back from the touch of surf
Toward makepiece fields. Toward cities where the wheel
Is dragging the horse by the whites of his eyes.
Islands draw in toward sacred places
Among clots of pines where the old stones are broken
Into stones that gleam like the first hour
As they are lofted into heaven.

Without air we die sooner; later without water;
But sooner or later we die without stone.
We cannot think of self without air and water.
We cannot think of God without stone.
And the rest is fire burning where the stones
Of the temple press together, or where the grains
Of the skin groan together as they rise
By their weight into heaven.

I saw the body of fire in the seams of
The temple. And I saw the stones grow old again
And settle once more into the horizon's

31

Memory. I walked the horizon, a circle
Between surf and a sacred center,
Measuring the race course where I had won
No race, my stride being that of any other man's:
An angle extended to infinity from the genitals.
At last in the silence of the circle, where
I asked no question, the answer escaped
From the sameness of the smoke rising with oracles.

The fire at the knee or the knuckle glitters
In the stately circle where you wheel
Again toward the mother's milk you spewed
Across the sky. A god returns to
His vomit. He is set there like the cold facture
Of a verse in a stranger's anthology.
Or, if you prefer, as a series of imaginary lines
Drawn between arbitrary stars not very
Far from the clutter of childhood.

# The Graiae

As the sun goes blind,
Those ladies pass from hand to hand
The gift of vision. They mew, cluck
And totter together, perhaps as a trick
To tempt whatever man is near
To steal what they cannot bear
To give him, and must. I cannot say
If the gift is the same for all.
I cannot even say what my own
Gift is. But it seems an acorn
With an improbably grandiose coronal,
And near the tip a neat hole
Where a worm went out or in.
Gramercy, ladies. Whatever it is
It nicely dots my eye, my I, my aye.

## *Fireflies*

Through fruity ooze
Of summer vespers, fireflies
Annotate their glide
With a luminous splurge.
Oh! punctate sketches of Cassiopeia's Chair.

The peasant of Euboea
Calls the firefly "arse-fire."

In another language that matters
Fireflies are the ghosts
Of Alexander Pope's pheasants
Who died in mid-air.

# *Snow*

Late snows spun from May rain come
Down heavy, wrecking tulips, breaking fruit
Trees. A gray sun stares at the fallen kindling wood.
But early snows, slanting in on autumn, shear
The trees of their burning fleece and, lying in
    the stubble, calm
It to pools of sulphur where sunlight comes to dream
Of the holy book it read on its long journey here.

# Museum of Natural History

Here it is, the world of the museum. The view
Is square within the round of vision. Behind glass
Each leaf seems to have been glued
On transparencies at different depths. Nevertheless
The illusions are relaxing. In a fake
Distance—but distance is not convenient—the Grand
Tetons, curled like chrysanthemum petals, break
A pseudo sky—but sky is after all a bore. And,
At any rate, the interest of the panorama
Is the foreground where in the tromped-on
Meadow above specimens of *primula incana*
Two bull elk, varnish fierce upon their horns,
Lunge toward each other with prosthetic glares.
They only fail to touch because the air
Between them is compressed to quartz
By their wild charge. In the world
This side of the glass, their horns would lock
And their legs churn until the meadow cracked
Between them and primulas fell like souls
Into the widening abyss.
                    True, their world without hell
Cannot be saved. Yet it saves merely because
It never comes to its side of the glass
To stare through a distance fossil-ferned
All over with the prints of very small hands.

# The Ancient One

(For Theodore Haddin)

Three years of drouth; and melting snow
No longer journeyed through bedrock labyrinths
To surface mysteriously dimpled and run
Down canyons. Stones—which under water made
Faces—nosed from the creek beds
Into the chaos of separate stones,
Brown moss lapsing like wigs from them.
All the dragon life of water, mandibles
And jointed legs, scattered over sand
Like flecks of metal thrown from a lathe.
And trout, the life-shaped trout, they died;
The strict lace of their skeletons
Caught in brambles of willow roots.
Except: where one small spring rose from a hole
Like a navel in the Roman road of the stream bed.
Its water, trembling with the molten, new-born
Clarity formed in darkness, came
From depths that had not heard of the surface
Weather. It filled one pool before it went
Down again into the sand. And here
Three minnows, like three hyphens, faced the source.

Years after the drouth I found the spring again.
Its old water still tumbled the sand
Into a newer snow water which flowed
As if to say to the land that all was forgiven.

37

The stream was too high in the mountains,
Too far from roads for hatchery fish,
But I cut a willow and baited a hook.

I did not see the trout. Only a dark swell
On the surface, sand plumes drifting back
With the current, and the line elegantly broken.
But I had not come to see or catch the trout.
I came to lay the baited hook upon the water
As an offering. And that is the way it was taken.

## A Long, Hard Winter

Beyond the strange neutrality of a window,
Beyond the rent webs of trees I see
In a field giddied by driving snow,
The two horses strained face forward like prows
Into the storm. The way they stand,
Neck over neck and flank to flank,
You'd think they were life-long friends.
They are not. They are all indifferent
To each other. In any other weather they prefer
A half-field share that they will not share.

But this is winter gone beyond winter's reasons,
Useless now to any root or well; less a season
Than some deep humiliation; pointless unless
There is a point in making horses stand near
Those they'd not be caught dead with, before they are.

# Summer People

Each night they heard
Him, the porcupine, come and gnaw salt
From the old privy boards
In the wood pile, The methodical
Chomp jawed the whole night.
But they, summer people, were at first
Amused and in the morning liked
To find the ochre quills like odd blades
Of grass tilted in the Vermont grass.

Until one night a summer fog settled heavily
Through the valleys. Crows cawed softly
In plasmic dark. Dogs bayed
From distant farms, but farther, farther away,
The scream of some stalking beast
Came like jagged waves through the mist.

This time when the gnawing began
They did not say, "There's our friend again,"
But rose from the bed, the wife
Taking a lantern and he a poker from the stove.
The light flowered in the drifting molecules
Of water. But like a light in a cave all
Of it spread in a rigid cirque
Bounded beyond by nothing but dark.
And so, without warning the porcupine
Was suddenly with them, rattling its spines,
Clicking its teeth. The poker descended,

But as if nothing had happened
The porcupine still stood where it had.
Again the poker fell across its snout.
It neither attacked nor ran, but stood,
Shaking its quills, staring into the light.
And they, because they found themselves caught
In a role they did not want, played
The role utterly. Again and again the poker fell
Until at last it seemed the animal
Poured itself down into a pool of its own blood.
And they, summer people, stood in their globule of light,
    wondering
Why they were here and what they would find in the
    morning.

# The Wicked Dogs

As we came down the high ravine
Steepness tilted the April afternoon
To noon. The hoarded snow dunes
Trembled as if boiling; each grain
Growing brighter in its diminishing.
We walked in a realm of oiled boots
And wet denim, and the skin beneath clothes
Swam in snow water. In that
Same water swam the gleaming chaparral roots.
In that water buttercups were floating up
Like cold ideas of a sun through theorems of night.
We were far removed from an air too cold
To be warmed by a sun that burned in
Through our shirts, through our skin of snow
Water to our winter white skins.
All chills coiled
In all fevers, we toiled,
Certain of our naked joy singing
Like a firewinter beneath the woven world.

And then a herd of deer sprang
Across the trail and two dogs after.
One found the ham string, the other
The throat of a gravid doe.
Then they were gone, yelping, after the herd again.
We stood where the blood melted the snow
For a distance and then by snow was frozen.

We stood amazed to think that our neighbor's
Dogs who were called by silly names
And petted and fed from a tin
Would turn to this secret ecstasy,
Reddening their muzzles on a full belly.

We stood so close in our grief that
The wind blew our hair together.
I wonder whether
We should be shocked anew
If we saw it all again.
That was a long time ago.
That was three wars ago.

# Belgrade, November 23, 1963

Slowly the grief of the street
Overflows its banks, covering the curios
Carved to stare like children
At strangers. And quieting at last
Even the whisper of traveler's checks.

In embassies the dolorous silt moves under
The doors and over the chessmen scattered
On the floor of the chamber where the secret radio
Pauses puzzled in its narrow channel.

But the mere people in black float down the street,
Past their legislated churches
To the altar of the newsstand where
The newspaper, the ink still wet,
Lies in state. In the brown lignitic air
Impartially diffusing
The brassy anger of the sun,
They bend to kiss the ikon,
The picture wreathed in words,
Taking its wet-ink shadow into their faces.

I stand aside, chilled by that face
That could not really believe that life
Could be painful. I gaze from the hotel window
Until the bullets of my failure
Touch his success. And then I, too, can grieve.
I, too, can join the mourners in their holy line.

44

I wear with them the turned-up shoes that remember
The Turkish lords. I wear their dark homespun robes.
I flow with them darkly on gondola shoes from Sarajevo
To Belgrade to Dallas. We move slowly with
The weight of our assassin's power, the triumph
Of our failure, the loss of our loss.
I take with them the ink stain on my mouth.
I bear the reversed words of the headline
On my brow, a shadow that every mirror
Will turn back into the blackest words.

# The Agora

After Belgrade's perfect justice
Which makes everyone suspicious
Of everyone else; after the equitable distribution
Of the shortages treasured by comrades, I totter gaga
And frowning into the market place of Salonica.

And then the music! I am drawn
By the cricket madrigals,
The baboon metric of hawkers. From prawns
Heaped like wet autumn leaves to barrels
Of olives staring like the unemployed through brine.
Wooed by heartbreak my heart beats again and I stop
Short where an azalea is blooming in a butcher shop.
I feel how the hand that sells a sprig of marjoram
Keeps in its nervous damp a zodiac of broken leaf
As a tea cup keeps some unlikely but beautiful fortune.

O wasteful ecstasy of the common agora, I pray
That in the social planners' city that soon will cover
The earth you will wickedly and always stay,
A chancy sprawl of unkempt brick. Sanctuary forever
Where those who are stupid can prove themselves clever;
And where those who—no matter what—
Will always be cheated, can cheat.

46

# Nestor's Palace

In these places of spent agonies
The grains of organic life,
Still fretful in the soil,
Swing, trembling, toward you
Like a compass needle.
They feel you as a hot tower
Of blood standing over them.
They hear the pulse
As thunder calling them back
To protoplasmic valleys.
And then their small voices, hardly able
To form words now, sing-song through
The medium of earth, making
The peevish gnat song that
Every life everywhere finally comes to.
It is always the same.
They whine against the unjust changes.
How the rooftree of the palace
Falls through barbarian flames
Upon the altars of the dozing gods.
How the tall jars of wine and oil—
With one strand of beads
Strewn like hysteria between them—
Squat debased in a coarse mosaic,
The palace returned now to its first idea,
A floor plan traced on the earth

Among anemones which are forever ignorant
Of the ninety ships to be sent to Troy.

I turn from the scene, leaving
A few skin cells, an eyelash, perhaps,
To add to these voices a modern lament:
"Someone's been sitting in *your* chair?"
My cells cry. "Someone's been sleeping
In *your* bed, you say? Well, someone's
Been making roads in *my* mountains,
My fragrant Wasatch. They have built
A road over my childhood!"

I turn, but as I turn I see in the far ocean
How an island
Was long ago changed by waves so that
One end stands separate, a black boar's tusk.
And I see where waves
Are thinning another place
So that in some distant time
Someone will pause amazed
By the beauty of two black
Tusks pointed toward the sky
In the always pearly but always shifting sea-light.

# Linear B

The dull Minoan scribe writes
"Eight jars of oil" on clay with a clumsy alphabet.
He is drawing to himself the long boats
Of the Mediterranean. They slue beneath the green walls
Of the trough. They rise like cumbrous birds,
Creaking on the slippery crest.
Sky, water, up, down, yet
Always drawing toward the jars of oil.
Toward the jars of oil they bear
The wordless parchment of the Nile,
The crude red gold of Asia. Century
By century they rise, yaw, fall, the crusted ropes
Heavy in the wind, yet always drawing
Toward the jars, bringing the wealth
That makes the shape of gods at last
Grow human and a little frail;
And bringing the power that frees the mind from power.
Then all is ready for the final cargo,
That flow of words, crying for the old or newer gods,
Nagging against the wealth and power that created them,
Pushing like a tide around the gray stones of the theatre.

All of this drawn forth by the words
"Eight jars of oil" written on clay
With a clumsy alphabet.

# Returning to Milan

Islands draw you with imperious singing to their rocks,
Then divorce you with gentle absent-mindedness. I took
A last look at the daughter, the son,
The sylph, the gnome, who had learned to speak
Their parts too well—and freed them into ruin.
I freed us all; broke the staff; buried the book;
And over seas of slag returned to Milan.

In this city of incidence, the light
Is hardly magic, hardly Prospero's. It is the flat
Touch of phenomenon. And what its neutral fingers
Touch is the boredom of whores, the orgasm of thieves
        and the hunger
Of those who are innocent. What the fingers write
On walls is that life will never be better than the
        sum of its parts.
But let's have it as it is. Let's take
Its knife to heart as by the shallowing lakes
We picnic on an overcrowded planet. Let us gaze
At the immune rose of a child's privileged face
As it glides embowered in an overpowered car
Through the city's brown sargasso of killing air.
Reverence the enigmatic rose that now prepares
To spurn the angels, pollute the stars and bear
Memories of islands into even deadlier atmospheres.

# Our Lady of Erice

This storm is rising from the mindless mind
Of flowers. From red gorse that wounds
Whole meadows. From stone crop whose blue eye blinds
The glaring rock. Most of all from marigold
Whose countless suns accomodate invasions from the field.
Marigold rises, a counter sunlight in the driving mist,
A brazen light that tells us how whatever is
Most passive and innocuous
Is what is finally most dangerous.

This storm rises from flowers! The sun goes behind
The wind, but the gold of Mary moves in the wind.
In the raging gold I cannot see the citadel
Above, nor the sea below the hill,
But I hear a nightingale raise its voice
In the old notes that descend in a shower on Zeus
As the virgin disguised as a virgin mocks
Him with the lullaby that keeps him awake.
And I hear the sailors answering from the sea
In drowned voices, crying, "We,
As death is our witness, Lady, sailed
Here before your temple was built
And after it crumbled, and what we came for, we got:
Your smile unchanged even though the flood
Arranged us. Your pallor unchanged by all our blood.
The knowledge that our knowledge was worth
Nothing unless it was worth our death.

The knowledge that what is worth nothing is
Worth death. Lady, we would not have it otherwise."

The mist, the bird, the voices burn away. The sun
Lies on the sea, a double sun cut by the gray horizon,
Hopelessly divided and dividing like a cell burled
On the womb-wall that is always and forever the world.

## The Pedagogue at Colonus

As he tries to tell
Them what befalls
Young Oedipus at Thebes, they smile
As their fingers scowl
To put
It all in notes.

But when he tries to tell
Them what befalls
Old men, he is all at once alone.
Chorus master without chorus
He stands in the empty theatre in Argos,
Speaking to the stone seats
On which the notes
Are already writ
By sediments
(Like snowblind footprints)
Of lime; and stains
(Like an old man's wayside piss)
Of iron.

## *Self-Land*

The distant knowledge of myself is of a land
With roads, beehives and alfalfa fields
Stretched cautiously in summer storms. But they end
At a high lake, and I'm suddenly aware
The element is new. I need claws or wings or gills
To get me over catastrophic shifts. For here
This lake refuses color from the sky but takes the leaden
Glance of granite peaks. Up these peaks somehow I must go.

How in that same fire that has melted my snow maiden
Can I ascend, grow diadems of frost, scepter of snow?

# The Beginning

Bent by wind the grass points
Toward destinations, now desert, now mountain.
In deserts I hear the hermetic cries
That, after birds have turned to little scabs
On stones, linger in space to die
In the disbelief of ears. In mountains, flowers
That have been eternal pass like ghosts
Back into their corpses, heave from the glacial shale
And show the long white hair of their roots.
These are beauties. They are also lies,
My way of shaking birds and flowers
From their idiocy. But I sicken myself by trying.
That is one way of putting it. There is another.

The clouds go over like years, and the wind
That drives them is not the wind that bends the grass.
"Where shall we go today?" asks grass and points
A way. "We go," say clouds. "This way," says grass.
"Yes, that is the way," say clouds, going another way.
Meantime, the stars ride the centuries through
The vacuum where a greater wind has run.

Come, my darlings, my humans, we have gotten
A little out of nature and cannot go its way.
We must find another wind to be faithful to.

# *Where We Are Going*

When the old lava came down
To this shore
It killed. Now algae like fern
And the vulnerable little jellies
Of life cling
To its wrinkles.

We, too, would like to cling.
But it is late, too late.

Out to sea
Three islands
Stand opaque and blue
In the pale glare.
Then the light
Works under them,
And they rise from the sea
To float in air.

Islands in the air?

The sea did it,
You say, with its mirrors.
True. But everything must
Be done with mirrors, my dear,
Whether the sea's or ours,
Everything seen with mirrors.

And it is too late now
To see it otherwise.
Our tall-masted yacht
Has left the old shore,
And are we not already sailing
Into the blinding light
Under the islands?

## Stansbury Island, Great Salt Lake

This island rises from water that coaxes no grasses
But traces, where it touches, the white scheme
That marries derelict truck tires to a gull's skeleton.
Only a little below the surface you see
The water doing its work, the cloudy moil
Where the salt continuously forms, the crystals growing
And homing downward in the plasmic roil.

Even the irrelevant life of the water—
The minuscule shrimps are so far gone to salt
That their bright bodies will burst
In rain water. Even so, they cannot wait
To become only salt. Like ruby sand they wash
Up the shore line, millions of them, dead and stinking,
But in a day they are possessed
By their demon. They become elegant and final.

From the summit of this island's bemused cliff,
I sit and gaze at the far water, and a pain
At the base of my spine reminds
Me of the long lost tail that my nerves,
Alerted by the height, still command
To grasp a jungle branch. I put one hand
Against an ancient juniper whose roots hold
Together the rock they once broke.
The other hand strays to touch
The primitive buttercups that have settled

In the rich debris of the tree. Their sticky leaves
Close when I touch them
Like a baby's hands around my fingers.

I think we are not in fashion here, we three,
Where the fashion is to go by going.
We go by staying.
Hold, old tree. Hold, invisible tail.
Hold, little hands.

## Mountains Like Slate

In this moment while the sun
Still quells the flowering of stars,
These mountains become their naked dimension.
Spurge, stony outcrops, canyons,
Where glacial swans once
Floated slowly to their deaths, all disappear
Until mere perpendiculars
Stand, as thin and flat
As sheets of slate.

Why is it, my dear, that we gaze
With such adoration through our haze
Of birthdays at this accident
Of light, time and space?
It hardly returns our love,
But tells us that our humanness
At most is temporary ornament
Like canyons, stony outcrops, spurge
Upon the naked slate of the universe.

For a bit I think that what we see
Is that this indifferent simplicity
Which tolerated once will tolerate
Again. Indifference so great
Would not care if our aggregate
Of atoms reassembled in a billion years
To offer its unwanted love here
Again to mountains like cold slate.

But when I look into your eyes
I repent my soft hypothesis.
Not of birthdays but of birth
I think. Through what straits of chance we both
Have come: You born too soon, too small;
I blue, strangling in a caul.

Your eyes say it was never our duty
To be immortal but to be implausible,
To be the unnecessary accident in the beauty
Which were too perfect if accidents were not barely possible.
To gather then in our unimportant net
All the beautiful accidents, even this accident:
These mountains like mountains of slate.